Crafts for Kids Who Are Wild About
Outer Space

Crafts for Kids Who Are
WILD
ABOUT
OUTER SPACE

By Kathy Ross
Illustrated by Sharon Lane Holm

The Millbrook Press   Brookfield, Connecticut

For Greyson, who has always liked his space!—K.R.
For my mother, who gave me space—S.L.H.

Library of Congress Cataloging-in-Publication Data
Ross, Kathy (Katharine Reynolds), 1948–
Crafts for kids who are wild about outer space / Kathy Ross ; illustrated by Sharon Lane Holm.
p. cm.
Summary: Provides instructions for twenty projects, creating such things as a planet mobile,
constellation tack board, space helmet, moon buggy, pop-up alien puppet, and rocket pin.
ISBN 0-7613-0054-6 (lib. bdg.)   ISBN 0-7613-0176-3 (pbk.)
1. Handicraft—Juvenile literature. 2. Outer space in art—Juvenile literature.
3. Space vehicles in art—Juvenile literature. [1. Handicraft. 2. Outer space in art.
3. Space vehicles in art.] I. Holm, Sharon Lane, ill. II. Title.
TT160.R714225 1997
745.5—dc20 96–14303 CIP AC

Published by The Millbrook Press, Inc.
2 Old New Milford Road
Brookfield, Connecticut 06804

cL
3/98

Contents

• •

Whether you are just learning about outer space or have been dazzled by the mysteries of space for a long time, you will have fun with this book. You can make stars and planets, spaceships and astronauts, and even a few aliens and a robot. Let your imagination soar into space with these ideas for projects you can make yourself.

Pom-Pom Planet Mobile

Here is what you need:

wire hanger
black construction paper
sticker stars
blue glue gel
scissors
blue yarn
pipe cleaner
pen

pom-poms for each of the planets:

The nine large bodies that orbit the sun are called planets. They are Mercury, Venus, Earth, Mars, Jupiter, Saturn, Uranus, Neptune, and Pluto.

Mercury:
1/2-inch (1.3-cm)
gray

Venus:
1-inch (2.6-cm)
yellow

Earth:
1-inch (2.6-cm)
blue

Mars:
1-inch (2.6-cm)
red

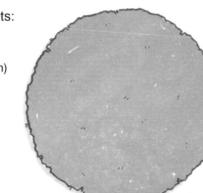

Jupiter:
2-inch (5-cm)
orange

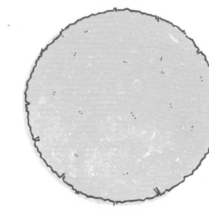

Saturn:
2-inch (5-cm)
yellow

Uranus:
1 1/2-inch
(4-cm) green

Neptune:
1 1/2-inch
(4-cm) blue

Pluto:
1/2-inch (1.3-cm)
gray

Here is what you do:

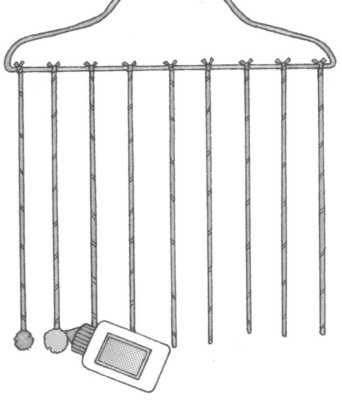

Cut nine pieces of yarn 14 inches (36 cm) long. Tie one end of each piece of yarn along the bottom of the coat hanger.

Starting at the left end of the hanger, glue a pom-pom planet to the end of each piece of yarn. Glue the planets in the order listed above, so that Mercury is at the far left of the hanger and Pluto is at the far right. This is the order of the planets from the sun. Glue a pipe-cleaner ring around Saturn, Uranus, and Neptune (although these planets have more than one ring). Let the glue dry.

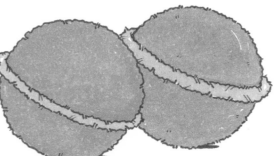

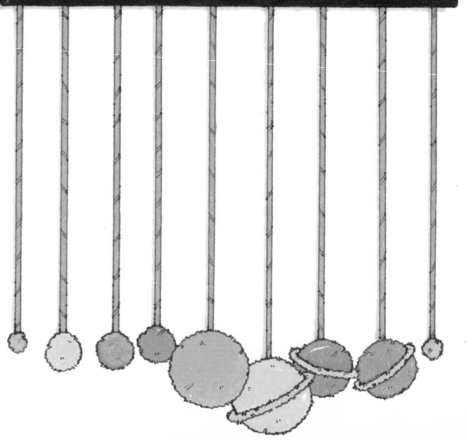

 Trace around the hanger with a pen on a sheet of black construction paper. Do not trace around the hook. Put another sheet of black paper underneath the tracing and cut around the traced line through both sheets. Put glue and the hanger between the pieces of paper so that the hanger—but not the hook—is completely covered.

Decorate the black paper with sticker stars to make it look like the night sky.

Can you name all the planets on your planet mobile?

Comet Ball

Here is what you need:

aluminum foil
thin Mylar ribbon
other colored ribbons
scissors

A comet is made up of rock, dust, ice, and gas. As a comet travels around the sun, it will often have a long "tail" of gases and dust streaming out behind it.

Here is what you do:

Tear off a large square of aluminum foil. Squeeze the foil together in the middle.

Tie four or five 30-inch-long (76-cm) pieces of ribbon around the foil so that the ends of each ribbon hang down to form the comet's tail.

Squeeze the foil on each side of the ribbon where the ribbon is tied to the foil. Keep wrapping and squeezing layers of aluminum foil around the ball until it is the size you want the comet to be. A ball that is about 2 inches (5 cm) in diameter seems to "fly" well.

Throw the comet ball and watch the colorful tail stream out behind it.

Flip-the-Rings-on-Saturn Game

Here is what you need:

tennis ball
orange tissue paper
white glue
yarn
disposable plastic bowl and craft stick
two plastic containers as wide as you would
   like your rings to be
Styrofoam tray
scissors
newspaper to work on

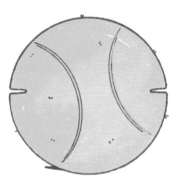

The planet Saturn is surrounded by rings made up of dust, rock, and ice that circle the planet.

Here is what you do:

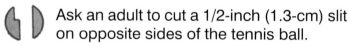 Ask an adult to cut a 1/2-inch (1.3-cm) slit
on opposite sides of the tennis ball.

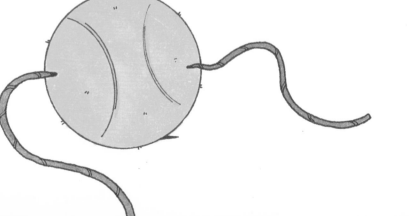

Cut a piece of yarn about 2 feet (61 cm) long.
String the yarn through one slit in the tennis
ball and out the other slit so that one end of the yarn
hangs out of each side of the ball.

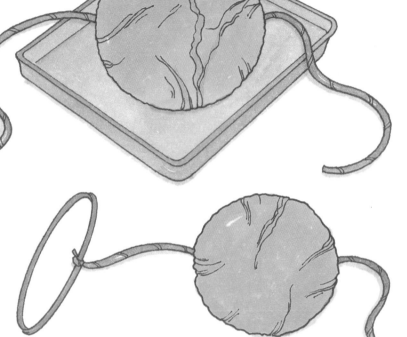

In the plastic bowl, mix about 2 ounces (58 ml) of glue with a small amount of water in the plastic bowl. Use the craft stick to stir the water into the glue.

Cut a piece of orange tissue paper large enough to cover the tennis ball. Dip the tissue in the watery glue and wrap it around the ball. Be sure to leave the two ends of the yarn free. Put the ball on the Styrofoam tray to dry.

Cut two rings for the ball from the rim of the two different-sized containers. Tie a ring to the end of each piece of yarn.

Flip the Rings on Saturn!

Can you flip the rings on Saturn? The smaller ring will be harder to flip on than the larger ring.

Starry-Sky Light Catcher

Here is what you need:

4-inch-diameter (10-cm) plastic lid
white glue
blue food coloring
paper cup
craft stick
blue yarn
aluminum foil
star-shaped hole punch
scissors
gold glitter
newspaper to work on

Each of the stars that fill the sky is made up of hot gases.

Here is what you do:

Pour about 4 ounces (118 ml) of glue into the paper cup. Add two or three drops of blue food coloring. Mix the glue and coloring well with the craft stick until the glue is an even color of blue.

Pour enough glue into the plastic lid to completely fill it.

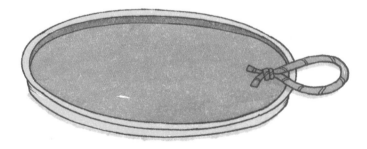

3) Cut a 3-inch-long (8-cm) piece of yarn. Press the two ends of the yarn into the glue at the edge of the lid to make a hanger.

4) Punch stars from the aluminum foil and set them on top of the glue. (If you do not have a star punch, you can cut the stars with scissors or use packaged sticker stars.) Sprinkle gold glitter over the top of the stars and glue.

5) Let this project dry for several days on a flat surface. When it is completely dry, peel the glue out of the plastic lid.

Hang your starry sky in a sunny window.

Constellation Tack Board

Here is what you need:

three Styrofoam trays of the same size
package of thumbtacks
package of gold star stickers
masking tape
white glue
white paper
black marker
scissors
pictures of different constellations

The stars form patterns in the sky called constellations. Each of the constellations has a name.

Scorpius, the Scorpion

Here is what you do:

1 Stick a gold star on the head of about 20 thumbtacks.

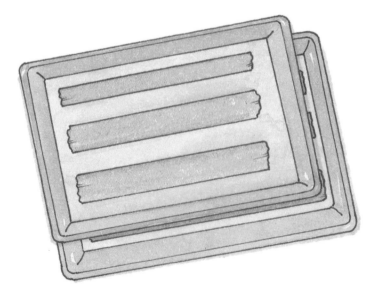

2 Put strips of masking tape on top of one tray and on the bottom of another. Put glue over the tape and press the trays together. Glue sticks more easily to masking tape than to Styrofoam.

Put strips of masking tape and glue on the bottom of the third tray and on top of the top stacked tray. Glue the third tray to the stack.

Cut sheets of white paper so that they will fit inside the top tray. Draw the star pattern of a different constellation on each sheet of paper. Be sure to write the name of the constellation under each drawing.

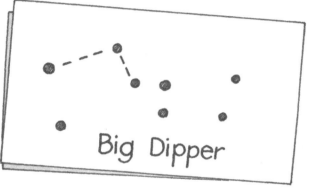

Big Dipper

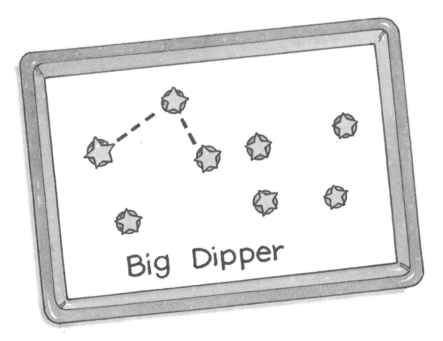

Big Dipper

Choose one of the constellation pictures and place it on top of the stacked trays. Push star tacks into the drawing to make the stars in the constellation. With this tack board and your pictures of the different constellations, you will quickly learn the star patterns so that you can recognize them in the sky.

Orbiting Sputnik

Here is what you need:

heavy 10-inch (25-cm) paper plate
cereal-box cardboard
brown construction paper
blue poster paint and a paintbrush
paper fastener
white glue
masking tape
1-inch (2.5-cm) Styrofoam ball
four toothpicks
aluminum foil
newspaper to work on

A satellite is an object that moves around a larger object. Sputnik 1, made by the Soviet Union in 1957, was the first artificial satellite in outer space.

Here is what you do:

Paint the bottom of the plate blue and let it dry completely.

Cut shapes of the continents from the brown paper and glue them on the blue plate. The plate will now look like the planet Earth.

Cut an 8-inch-long (20-cm) strip of cardboard. Make the strip about 2 inches (5 cm) wide at one end and about 1/2 inch (1.3 cm) wide at the other end. Attach the wide end to the center of the unpainted side of the plate with a paper fastener. The strip should spin freely around the plate when you push it with your finger.

4 To make the satellite, cut the Styrofoam ball in half. Cut the four toothpicks so that they are 1½ inches (4 cm) long. Push them into the Styrofoam ball half, evenly spaced and at an angle, so that they form the antennas for the satellite.

5 Cover the satellite and antennas with aluminum foil.

6 Put a piece of masking tape on the flat side of the satellite to help the glue to stick. Glue the satellite to the end of the cardboard strip. As you move the strip, the satellite will orbit the Earth.

Compare your satellite to pictures of the real Sputnik 1, which you can find in an encyclopedia.

Astronaut-into-the-Spaceship Puppet

Here is what you need:

cardboard paper-towel tube
bathroom-size paper cup
blue yarn
white paper
white glue
markers
masking tape
yarn, rickrack, and ribbon
scissors
aluminum foil
cereal-box cardboard
cellophane tape
red and blue sticker stars

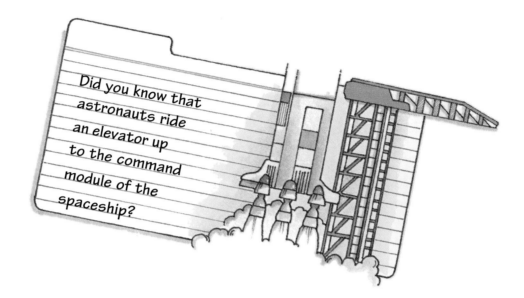

Did you know that astronauts ride an elevator up to the command module of the spaceship?

Here is what you do:

In one end of the tube, cut out a piece of cardboard 1 inch (2.5 cm) wide and 4 inches (10 cm) long. Tape the paper cup over the cut end of the tube to make the top of the rocket ship, leaving a small cutout opening.

Cut two fins of the same shape and size for the bottom of the rocket. Cut a slit on each side of the bottom of the tube. Slide each fin into one of the slits so that the fins stick out on each side of the rocket. Tape the fins on the inside of the tube to hold them in place.

3 Cover the entire rocket ship with aluminum foil. Decorate the rocket with sticker stars. If you want to glue ribbon and other trims to the rocket, too, first place masking tape on the foil so the glue will stick.

4 Fold a sheet of white paper in half. Draw an astronaut about 1½ inches (4 cm) tall on the fold of the paper. Draw a little platform under the astronaut. Cut through both layers of the folded paper around the top, bottom, and one side of the astronaut. Be sure not to cut away the fold.

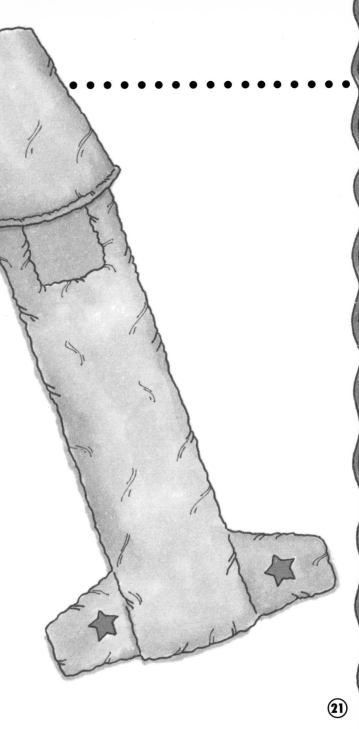

5 Cut a piece of blue yarn about 2 feet (60 cm) long. String the yarn through the opening in the top of the rocket and out the bottom. Tie the ends of the yarn together so that it forms a loop.

6 Open the folded astronaut picture, wrap it around the yarn, and glue the front and back of the picture together.

Pull the yarn to lift the astronaut up and into the spaceship.

Stars-in-a-Jar Shaker

Here is what you need:

small clear jar with screw-top lid
corn syrup
aluminum foil
star-shaped hole punch
masking tape
thin blue ribbon
blue food coloring
water

Bring a little bit of outer space right into your house with this mysterious star shaker.

Here is what you do:

1. Fill the jar almost to the top with corn syrup. Add a few drops of blue food coloring.

2. Punch eight or more stars from aluminum foil with a star-shaped hole punch. If you do not have a star punch, use a round hole punch. These "stars" will look pretty, too, but punch more of them because they are smaller. Put the stars in the corn syrup.

3. Add water to the jar to fill it. Put the lid tightly on the jar. Shake the jar to color the syrup evenly. Tape around the edge of the jar with masking tape. Cover the lid with aluminum foil. Tie a blue ribbon around the rim of the jar.

Shake and turn the jar and watch the stars float slowly in outer space.

Moon Buggy

Here is what you need:

old toy car about 6 inches (15 cm) long
cardboard egg carton
aluminum foil
masking tape
cellophane tape
white glue
plastic flexi-straw
pry-off bottle cap
two thumbtacks
foil cupcake wrapper

Astronauts traveled in a Lunar Rover to explore the moon. Make your own version of a vehicle that can travel on the surface of the moon.

Here is what you do:

1) Cut the egg carton in half. Each half should have two rows of three cups. One half of the carton will be the top of the buggy. Cut two egg cups out of the other half and set the rest aside. Glue the two cups to one end of the first half egg carton. Let the glue dry and cover the half carton with aluminum foil.

2) Push a thumbtack in each of the two bumps at the front of the buggy to make the headlights.

3) Cut two cups from the other half of the egg carton. Cut a piece out of the sides of each cup to make seats. Put the seats in the two cups behind the headlights. Put masking tape over the foil to help the glue stick, then glue the seats in place.

4 Put masking tape on the top of the bottle cap and on the foil in front of one of the seats. To make the steering wheel, glue the cap to the tape-covered foil in front of the seat.

5 Cover the top of the toy car with aluminum foil. Put strips of masking tape and glue on the top of the car and on the bottom of the moon buggy. Glue the car and buggy together. Now the buggy has wheels and can roll around.

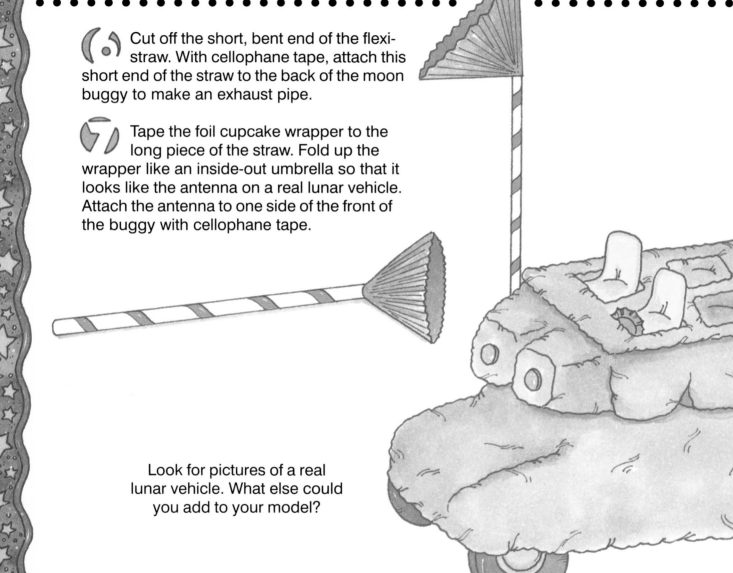

6. Cut off the short, bent end of the flexi-straw. With cellophane tape, attach this short end of the straw to the back of the moon buggy to make an exhaust pipe.

7. Tape the foil cupcake wrapper to the long piece of the straw. Fold up the wrapper like an inside-out umbrella so that it looks like the antenna on a real lunar vehicle. Attach the antenna to one side of the front of the buggy with cellophane tape.

Look for pictures of a real lunar vehicle. What else could you add to your model?

Straw Rocket

Here is what you need:

plastic drinking straw
sheet of typing paper
scissors
cellophane tape
marker
white glue

Here is what you do:

Here is a rocket to make and launch yourself.

U.S.A

1) Cut the typing paper so that it fits around the straw. Wrap the paper loosely around the straw and tape it in place. The paper should slide on and off the straw easily.

2) Slide the paper off the straw. Fold one end of the paper tube into a point to form the nose of the rocket. Hold the point in place with tape.

3) Cut two triangle-shaped fins for the bottom of the rocket. Put the paper rocket between the fins and glue them together.

4) Use a marker to write the name of your rocket down one side.

To launch your rocket, slide it down over one end of the straw. Blow on the other end of the straw and watch the rocket soar.

Rocket Pin

Here is what you need:

old necktie
gold rickrack
gold trim
alphabet pasta
blue glue gel
safety pin

Rocket ships carry astronauts and equipment through outer space. This little rocket is a blast to wear!

Here is what you do:

Cut a 3-inch-long (7.7-cm) piece off the thin, pointed end of the necktie. This piece will be the rocket.

Cut three pieces of gold rickrack and two pieces of gold trim about 2½ inches (6 cm) long. Glue the ends of the rickrack inside the cut end of the tie. They will look like fiery fuel coming out of the rocket.

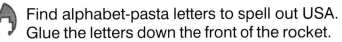 Glue a short piece of gold trim to decorate the bottom edge of the rocket.

Find alphabet-pasta letters to spell out USA. Glue the letters down the front of the rocket.

Attach a safety pin to the back of the rocket.

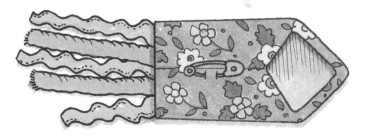

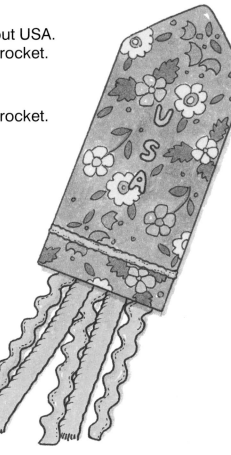

Let this rocket zoom across you or a friend!

Racing Rocket

Here is what you need:

large-size oatmeal box
blue 6-inch-wide (15-cm) plastic bowl
plastic drinking straw
cellophane tape
blue yarn
aluminum foil
hole reinforcers
permanent markers
orange tissue paper
stickers of people or animals

Take your doll friends for a ride in this racing rocket ship.

Here is what you do:

1 Cover the outside of the oatmeal box with aluminum foil to make the rocket ship. Tape the blue bowl to the bottom of the box to make the nose of the ship. Stick hole reinforcers around the sides of the bowl so that they look like portholes.

2 Use the black marker to draw windows on each side of the rocket. Put stickers of faces in the windows so that a passenger peeks out of each window.

3) Tuck a 12-inch (30-cm) square of orange tissue paper partway into the open end of the rocket so that it will look like flames are shooting out.

4) Tape the plastic straw to the top of the ship. Cut a piece of yarn about 14 feet (427 cm) long. String the yarn through the straw. Decorate the rocket using the permanent markers.

Tie the end of the yarn at the front of the ship to a sturdy chair or ask a friend to hold it for you. Pull the ship all the way to the other end of the yarn. Hold that end of the yarn as high as you can and give the rocket a push. Blast off! Make more than one of these rockets and have a rocket race!

Doll Friend Space Suit

Here is what you need:

small doll or stuffed animal willing to travel
aluminum foil
paper cup or cardboard tube that fits
   over the doll's head
plastic wrap
black pipe cleaners
small jewelry box
paper fasteners
scissors
cellophane tape
red and blue sticker stars

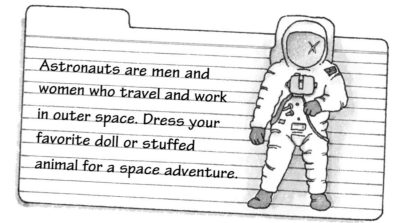

Astronauts are men and women who travel and work in outer space. Dress your favorite doll or stuffed animal for a space adventure.

Here is what you do:

1. Make a helmet for the doll by cutting a face hole in the cup or cardboard tube. If you are using a cardboard tube, you may need to cut it so that it is short enough to fit over just the doll's head. Cut a small piece of plastic wrap. Tape it inside the helmet to cover the face hole and make a clear face mask.

2. Cover the helmet and the body of the doll with aluminum foil to make the space suit. Be sure not to cover the face hole.

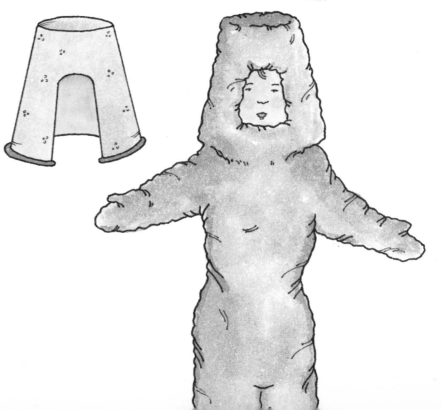

 Next, make an air pack for the astronaut to carry. On each side of the box, thread a piece of pipe cleaner through the top and bottom to make shoulder straps. Put paper fasteners into the lid of the box to make knobs on the air pack. Put the air pack on the doll. Put one end of another pipe cleaner inside the box and the other end in front of the face mask to make an air hose for your astronaut to breathe through.

4 Decorate the astronaut suit with red and blue sticker stars.

Make the Racing Rocket on page 30 and give your doll friend a ride.

Space Helmet

Here is what you need:

two large brown grocery bags
clear plastic deli container
white poster paint and a paintbrush
scissors
white glue
masking tape
plastic gallon milk jug
white paper
pencil
markers
newspaper to work on

Astronauts must wear special equipment like this space helmet to survive in outer space.

Here is what you do:

Put one of the grocery bags inside the other to make a double bag. Cut enough off the ends of the bags so that they fit over your head and rest on your shoulders like a helmet. The bottoms of the bags rest on the top of your head.

To make the clear face mask in the helmet, you can use either a round or rectangular plastic container. Near the top of one of the wide sides of the bags, trace around the bottom of the plastic container with the pencil. Carefully cut through the two bags to cut out the traced shape. Slide the plastic container

between the two bags. The bottom of the container should stick out to form the front of the face mask. The edges of the container should be between the two bags. Tape the edges to hold them in place. Rub glue in between the two bags to hold them together and keep the face mask in place.

 Paint the outside of the bags white. Place the helmet over a plastic jug to dry.

Ч When the helmet is dry, draw an American flag on white paper and cut it out. Glue the flag to one side of the helmet.

You can add the letters USA or the letters of your name to decorate your space helmet, too.

Weightless Box

Here is what you need:

cardboard box with a clear plastic lid
aluminum foil
masking tape
black permanent marker
blue yarn
cardboard egg carton
white glue
four Styrofoam packing peanuts
a tissue

Astronauts in outer space are weightless.

Here is what you do:

1. Cover the entire inside and outside of the box with aluminum foil. The inside of the box is the inside of a spaceship.

2. Cut four cups from the cardboard egg carton. Cut the sides off two of the cups. Glue the bottom of one cut cup to the bottom of an uncut cup to make a chair. Make two chairs.

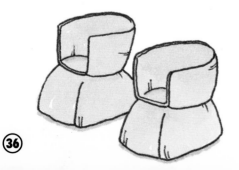

3. Stand the box on its side. Put two strips of masking tape along the bottom edge and glue the two chairs to the tape.

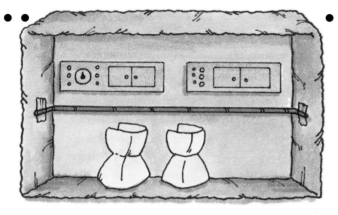

 Tape a yarn railing across the box, above and behind the chairs. When the astronauts are weightless, they will need the railing to hold on to and to pull themselves around the cabin of the ship.

5 Put strips of masking tape around the walls of the cabin. Draw control panels on the tape with the black marker.

6 Draw a face on each of the four Styrofoam peanuts. (I used two white ones for astronauts and two green ones for Martian passengers.) You can put as many passengers as you want in your rocket ship.

7 Place the lid on the box and tape it in place.

To make your astronauts and their passengers "weightless," rub the plastic quickly with a tissue. The static electricity this creates will make them float around in the spaceship cabin.

Magnetic Space Walk

Here is what you need:

shoebox
black poster paint and a paintbrush
magnet and magnetic bar
colored sticker stars
gray construction paper
black marker
cardboard toilet-tissue tube
bathroom-size paper cup
aluminum foil
white glue
masking tape
scissors
yarn
newspaper to work on

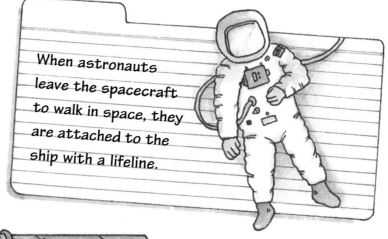

When astronauts leave the spacecraft to walk in space, they are attached to the ship with a lifeline.

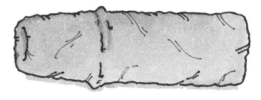

Here is what you do:

 Paint the inside of the shoebox with the black paint and let it dry.

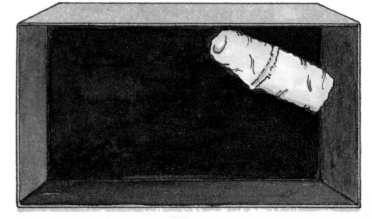 Tape the inside bottom of the cup to one end of the cardboard tube to make a rocket ship. Cover the rocket with aluminum foil. Decorate the ship with sticker stars. Put a strip of masking tape along one side of the ship. Glue the taped side of the ship at an angle pointed skyward to the inside of the black box.

Put gold and silver sticker stars all over the inside of the box to make it look like outer space.

On the gray paper, draw an astronaut about 2 inches (5 cm) tall. Cut out the astronaut. Cut a 12-inch (30-cm) piece of yarn. Glue one end of the yarn behind the spaceship in the box. Tape the other end of the yarn to the back of the astronaut. Tape the magnetic bar to the back of the astronaut.

To take the astronaut for a space walk, hold the magnet behind the box and move the astronaut around to explore outer space.

GIANT MAGNET

Command Module and Parachute

Here is what you need:

bathroom-size paper cup
aluminum foil
blue yarn
star stickers
scissors
plastic grocery bag
hole punch
four hole reinforcers
black permanent marker

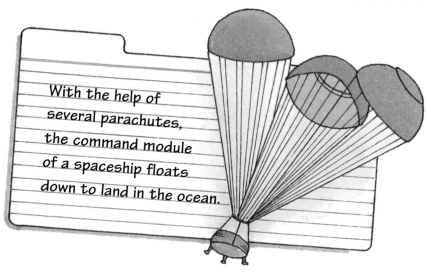

With the help of several parachutes, the command module of a spaceship floats down to land in the ocean.

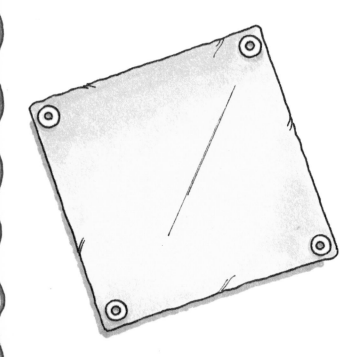

Here is what you do:

To make the parachute, cut a 12-inch (30-cm) square from the plastic grocery bag. Punch a hole in each corner of the square. Cover the outer edges of each hole with a reinforcer.

Cover the outside of the cup with aluminum foil. This will be the command module. Draw a window on the side of the module with the black marker. Add the face of an astronaut looking out. Decorate the module with some star stickers. Poke a hole in the top of the module.

Cut four 12-inch-long (30-cm) pieces of yarn. Tie an end of each piece of yarn to each of the four corners of the parachute. String the other ends of the yarn through the hole in the top of the module. Knot the ends together inside the cup to keep them from slipping back through the hole.

Toss your module into the air and watch the parachute lower it gently to safety.

Pop-Up Alien Puppets

Here is what you need:

two 6-inch (15-cm) disposable plastic bowls
two 12-inch (30-cm) pipe cleaners
old knit glove
masking tape
scissors
light-colored felt scrap
sharp, black permanent marker
blue glue gel
hole punch

These little aliens, creatures from outer space, pop out of their flying saucer to have a look around.

Here is what you do:

To make the flying saucer, put the rim of one bowl on top of the rim of the other bowl. Cut two pieces of pipe cleaner 3 inches (8 cm) long. Poke a hole in the rim of the top bowl. Then poke a hole in the rim of the bottom bowl directly below the top hole.

Thread one piece of pipe cleaner through both of the holes and twist the two ends together to form a hinge. Poke another set of holes about 2 inches (5 cm) away from the first set and make another pipe-cleaner hinge.

Cut the bottom out of the bottom bowl. Stick squares of masking tape around the sides of the top bowl of the saucer to make windows.

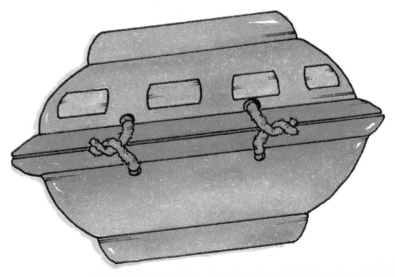

Each of the five fingers of the glove will be a little alien. Cut five 1½-inch-long (4-cm) pieces of pipe cleaner. Thread a piece through the tip of each finger of the glove. Bend the ends to make antennas for each alien.

Punch ten holes from the felt to make eyes for the aliens. Make a pupil in the middle of each eye with the black marker. Glue a pair of eyes to the front of each finger.

Put the glove on your hand and put your hand through the hole in the bottom of the saucer. Keep your fingers folded down. Push your hand upward and open your fingers to pop the aliens out of their flying saucer.

Alien-in-a-Saucer Necklace

Here is what you need:

small twist-on flip-top from a toothpaste tube
plastic or metal twist-on cap from a soda bottle
cotton swab
two tiny wiggle eyes
yarn
aluminum foil
masking tape
white glue
scissors
green poster paint
Styrofoam tray

"Take me to your leader...."

Here is what you do:

 Dip one end of the cotton swab in green paint. Let it dry on the Styrofoam tray.

 Cover the outside of the twist-on cap with masking tape. Cover the bottom edge of the flip-top with masking tape.

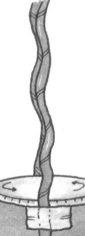 Cut a piece of yarn about 30 inches (76 cm) long to make the hanger for the necklace. Tie the yarn around the twist-on cap so that the ends are in the middle of the top of the cap. Tape the yarn on each side of the cap to hold it in place.

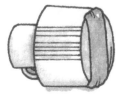

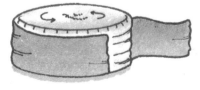

Rub glue over the masking tape on top of the cap. String the two ends of the yarn through the bottom of the flip-top. Slide the top down the yarn so that it meets the glue on top of the cap.

Cut off the green end of the painted cotton swab so that it is about 1 inch (2.5 cm) long. Dip the cut end in glue and slide it next to the yarn coming out of the top of the flip-top. Glue two tiny wiggle eyes to the front of the green swab. Let the project dry in the Styrofoam tray.

Cover the bottom and sides of the cap with a piece of aluminum foil, pressing it around the bottom edge of the flip-top.

Knot the two ends of the yarn together, and your alien friend is ready to wear around planet Earth.

Robot Hideaway

Here is what you need:

2-liter plastic soda bottle
small coffee can
scissors
aluminum foil
masking tape
white glue
nuts and bolts
gold glitter

Robots are machines built to help people with their work. This robot will help you stash your secret stuff.

Here is what you do:

With scissors, cut the bottle at the top where it starts to slant. The bottom of the bottle will be the top of the robot, so turn the bottle over.

Cover the robot with aluminum foil, folding the edges inside the open end. The robot should slip easily over the coffee can.

Choose some nuts and bolts to use as facial features for the robot. Put a small piece of masking tape on the back of each metal piece and on the places on the robot where you wish to glue the metal. The tape will provide a surface that the glue will stick to. If you have tape edges sticking out around the nuts and bolts, you can rub them with glue and sprinkle them with glitter.

Hide important things in the coffee can and slip the robot over the top of the can so that no one can find it. The robot will never tell!

About the author and illustrator

Twenty years as a teacher and director of nursery school programs have given Kathy Ross extensive experience in guiding young children through crafts projects. She lives in Oneida, New York.

Sharon Lane Holm won awards for her work in advertising design before shifting her concentration to children's books. Her illustrations have added zest to books for both the trade and educational markets. She lives in New Fairfield, Connecticut.

Kathy Ross and Sharon Lane Holm have also created the popular eight-book series Holiday Crafts for Kids, published by The Millbrook Press.